H

D0571033

LET'S PLAY
Hockey

Karen Durrie

www.av2books.com

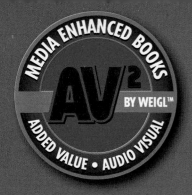

AV² MEDIA ENHANCED BOOKS
AV² BY WEIGL™
ADDED VALUE • AUDIO VISUAL

Go to www.av2books.com, and enter this book's unique code.

BOOK CODE

Q525466

AV² by Weigl brings you media enhanced books that support active learning.

AV² provides enriched content that supplements and complements this book. Weigl's AV² books strive to create inspired learning and engage young minds in a total learning experience.

Your AV² Media Enhanced books come alive with...

Audio
Listen to sections of the book read aloud.

Video
Watch informative video clips.

Embedded Weblinks
Gain additional information for research.

Try This!
Complete activities and hands-on experiments.

Key Words
Study vocabulary, and complete a matching word activity.

Quizzes
Test your knowledge.

Slide Show
View images and captions, and prepare a presentation.

... and much, much more!

Published by AV² by Weigl
350 5th Avenue, 59th Floor New York, NY 10118
Website: www.av2books.com   www.weigl.com

Durrie, Karen.
  Hockey / Karen Durrie.
    p. cm. -- (Let's play)
  ISBN 978-1-61690-940-6 (hardcover : alk. paper) -- ISBN 978-1-61690-586-6 (online)
  1. Hockey--Juvenile literature. I. Title.
  GV847.25.D87 2011
  796.962--dc23
                          2011023431

Printed in the United States of America in North Mankato, Minnesota
1 2 3 4 5 6 7 8 9 0 15 14 13 12 11

062011
WEP030611

Project Coordinator: Karen Durrie Art Director: Terry Paulhus

Weigl acknowledges Getty Images as the primary image supplier for this title.

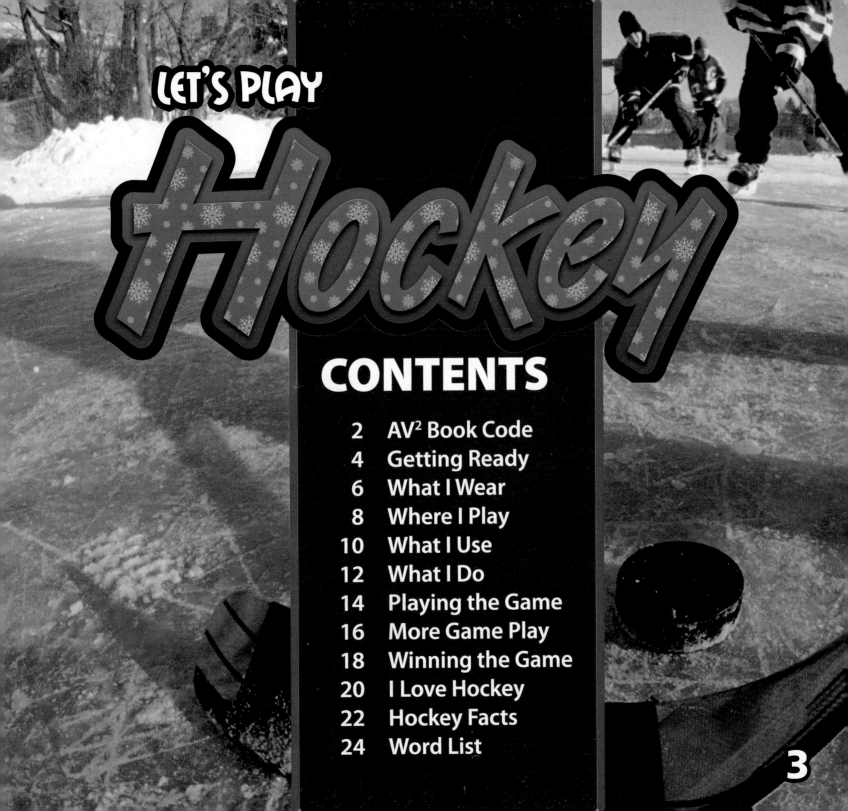

LET'S PLAY Hockey

CONTENTS

2 AV² Book Code
4 Getting Ready
6 What I Wear
8 Where I Play
10 What I Use
12 What I Do
14 Playing the Game
16 More Game Play
18 Winning the Game
20 I Love Hockey
22 Hockey Facts
24 Word List

I love hockey.
I am going to play
hockey today.

4

Hockey was first played on frozen lakes and rivers.

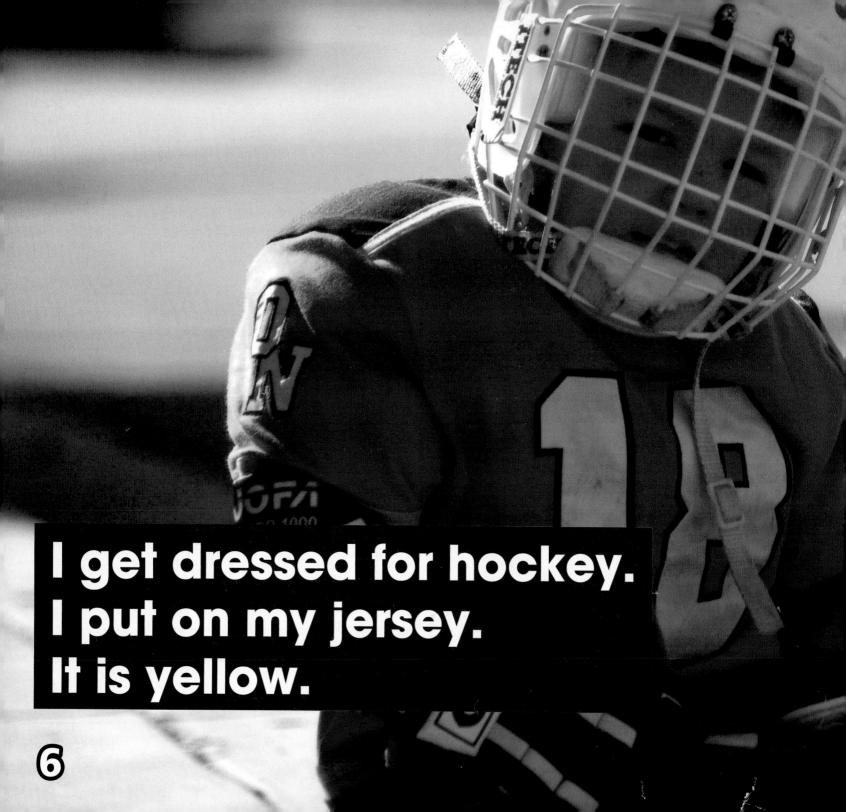

I get dressed for hockey.
I put on my jersey.
It is yellow.

Like a PRO

I wear pads
so I do not
get hurt.

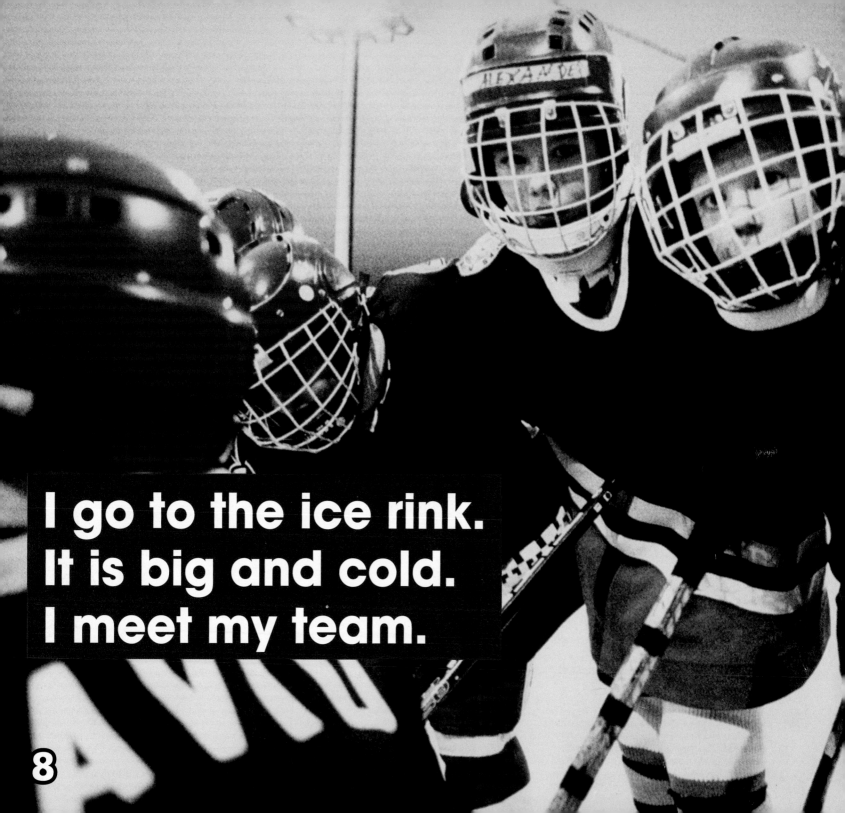

I go to the ice rink.
It is big and cold.
I meet my team.

8

An ice rink has pipes under the ice that keep it frozen.

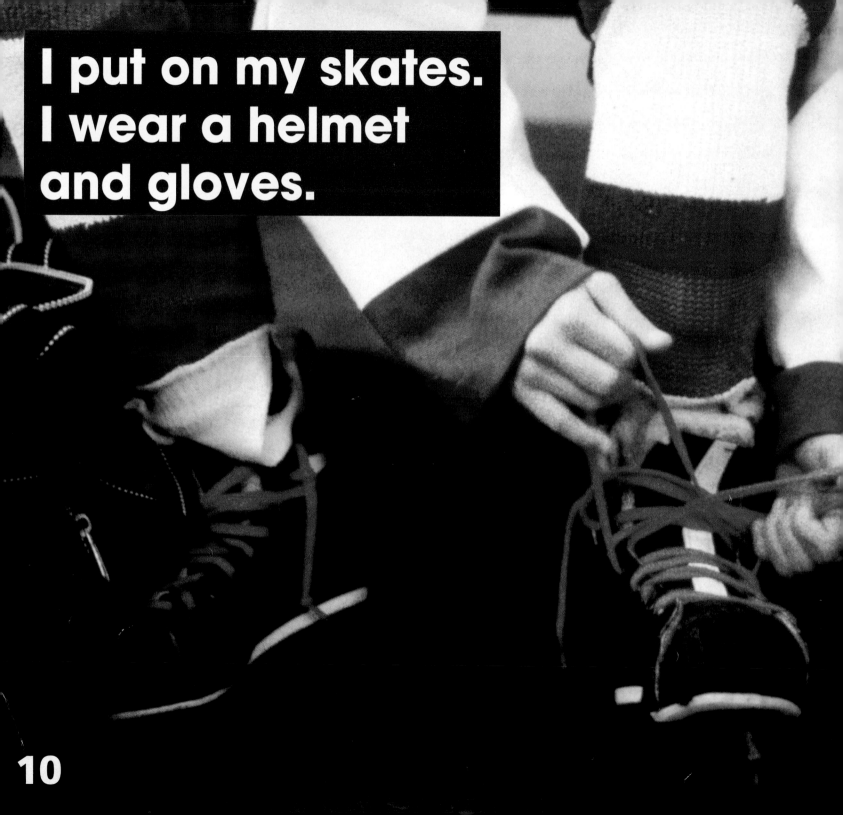

I put on my skates.
I wear a helmet
and gloves.

The blades on hockey skates slide quickly on ice.

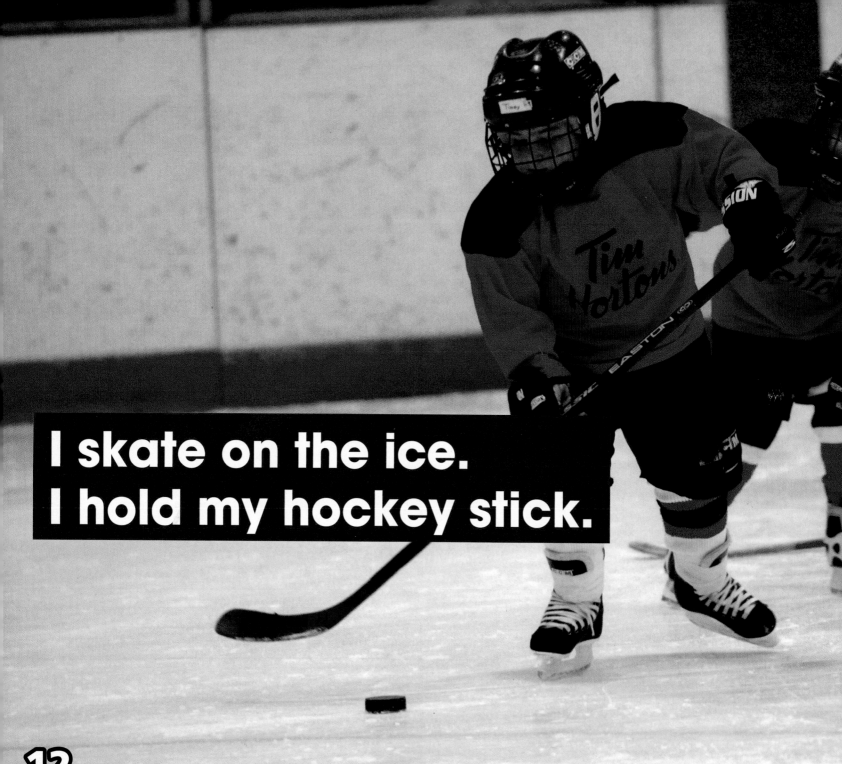

I skate on the ice.
I hold my hockey stick.

We skate
in circles.
This warms us
up to play.

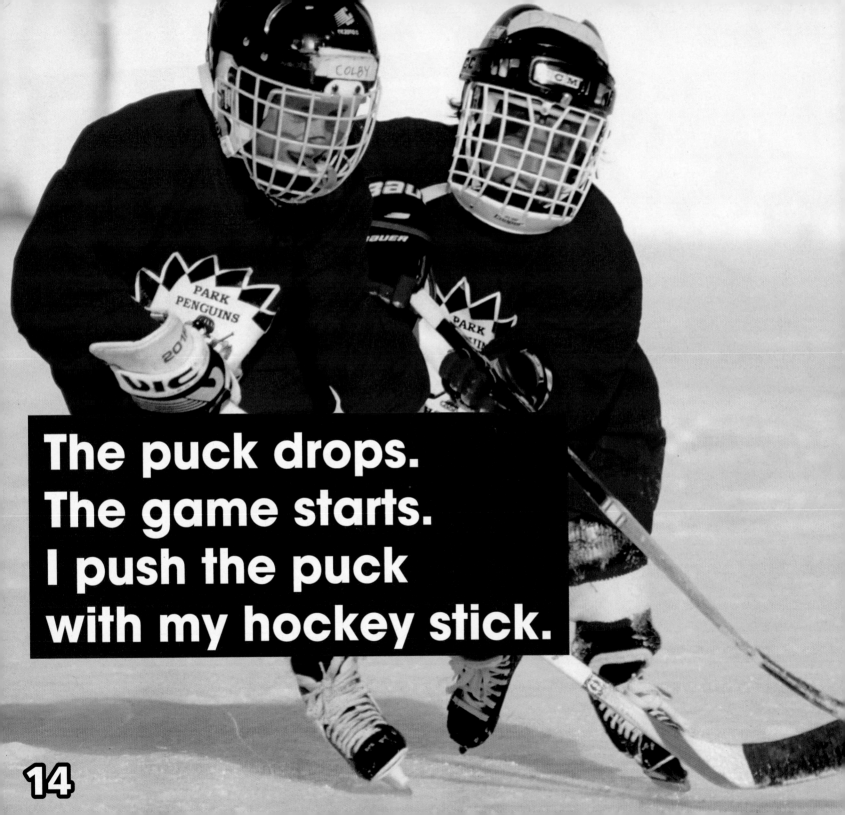

The puck drops.
The game starts.
I push the puck
with my hockey stick.

Holding my hockey stick helps me to balance.

I skate fast.
I pass the puck.
I move up the ice.

The coach tells us when to rest and when to play.

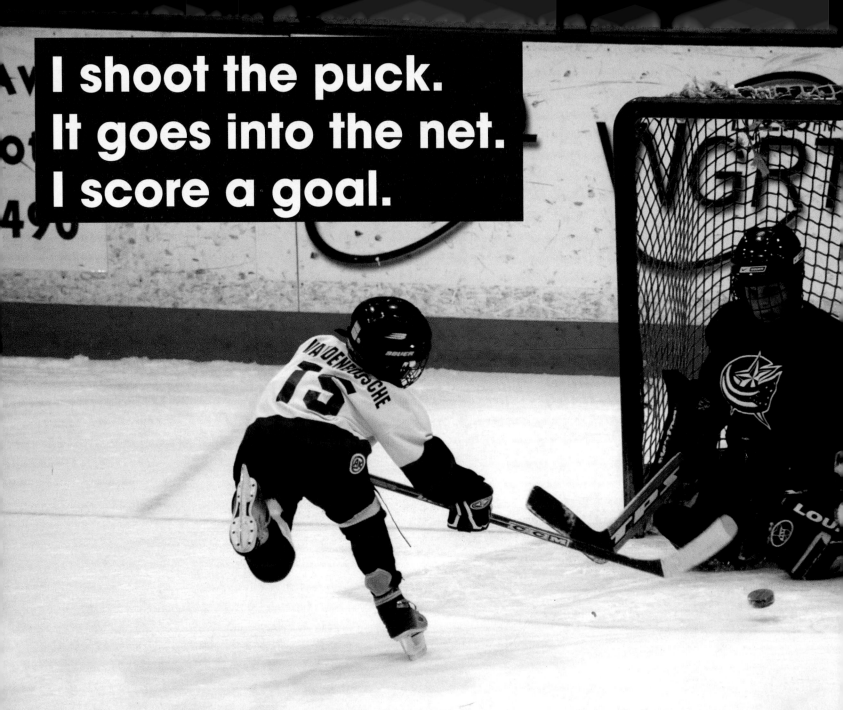

I shoot the puck.
It goes into the net.
I score a goal.

18

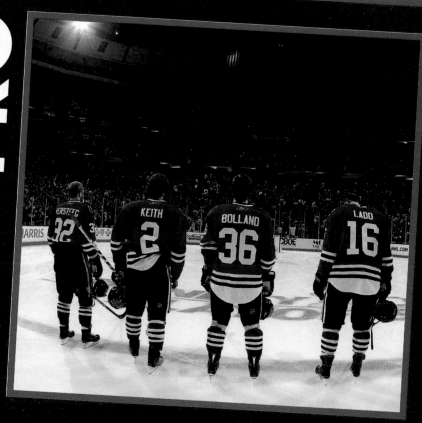

Teams work together to win a game. Every player has a job to do.

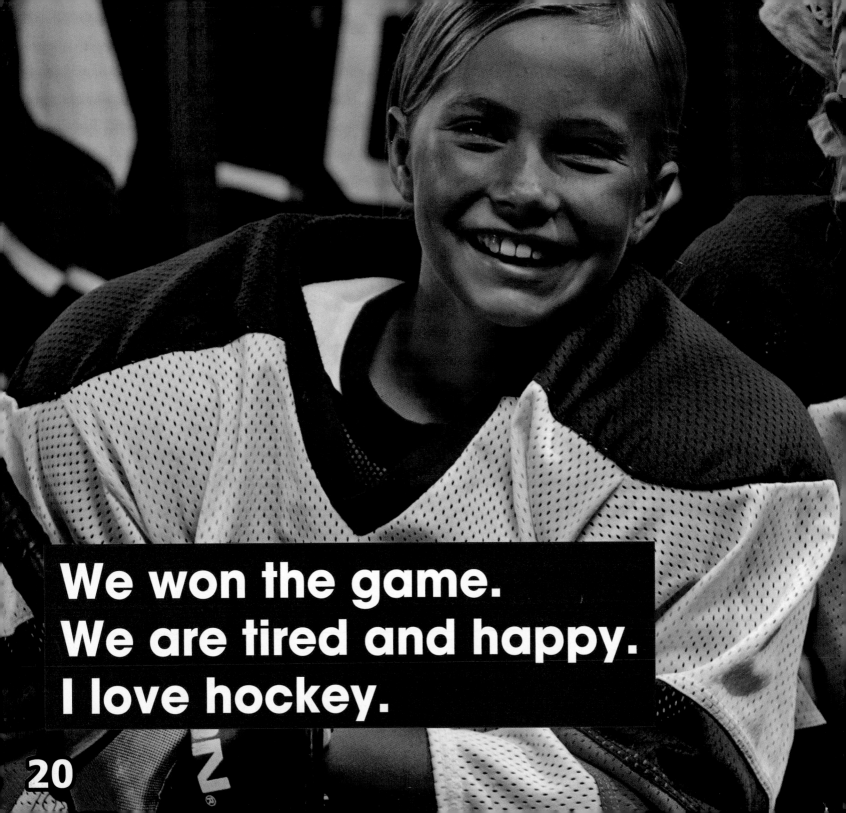

We won the game.
We are tired and happy.
I love hockey.

20

HOCKEY FACTS

This page provides more detail about the interesting facts found in the book.
Simply look at the corresponding page number to match the fact.

Pages 4-5

The word hockey comes from the French word "hoquet," which means "shepherd's crook." There are two teams in a hockey game. Each team tries to put the puck into the other team's net. The team that scores the most goals during the game wins.

Pages 6–7

Hockey requires a lot of gear. Hockey gloves protect the player's hands and keep them warm. Elbow and shoulder pads are worn beneath the jersey. Hockey pants are padded shorts, used for warmth and to protect players when they fall on the ice. Helmets may include wire face guards to prevent injury.

Pages 8–9

The hockey rink is a big sheet of ice that has a net at each end. High boards surround the ice to keep the players and the puck inside. Lines and circles painted on a layer beneath the ice are important to the game. The circles show where officials drop the puck to start play.

Pages 10–11

It takes some time to get skilled on skates. It is not easy at first to balance on the thin metal blades on a slippery surface. Gliding, skating very quickly, turning, stopping hard, changing directions, and skating backwards are all essential skills for playing hockey.

Pages 12–13

Cold muscles are stiff, and sudden twisting and turning of them can cause injury. Warming and stretching muscles before playing hockey can reduce the risk of injury. Warm muscles also produce more energy faster. This helps a player skate faster and perform with more accuracy and skill.

Pages 14–15

Hockey pucks are made from a compressed mixture of rubber, coal dust, and oil. Most hockey sticks are made of wood, but some are made of graphite, or a combination of graphite and fiberglass. Skating holding a hockey stick helps players with balance.

Pages 16–17

Hockey teams have more players than there are positions on the ice. The players that are not on the ice sit on players' benches that have special gates for going on and off the rink. The coach tells players when to come off and rest, and when to get on the ice and play.

Pages 18–19

It is exciting to score goals and win games, but learning new skills and enjoying your sport is also important. In hockey, working together as a team by passing the puck and setting up good shots helps a team be successful. If a hockey game is won, it is the team that wins, not just the players that scored goals.

Pages 20–21

Playing a sport involves gear and a special place to play. It also involves preparing the body to work hard. Eating healthy food helps fuel the body to do its best. Eating right makes bones stronger and gives muscles energy. A snack and drink after playing sports helps to replace the energy spent during a game.

WORD LIST

Research has shown that as much as 65 percent of all written material published in English is made up of 300 words. These 300 words cannot be taught using pictures or learned by sounding them out. They must be recognized by sight. This book contains 40 common sight words to help young readers improve their reading fluency and comprehension. This book also teaches young readers several important content words. These words are paired with pictures to aid in learning and improve understanding.

Page	Sight Words First Appearance	Page	Content Words First Appearance
4	I, play, to,	4	hockey, today
5	first, on, rivers, was	5	lakes, rivers
6	for, get, is, it, on, my, put	6	jersey
7	do, not, so, under	7	pads
8	and, big, go, the	8	ice, rink, team
9	an, has, keep, that	9	pipes
10	a	10	gloves, helmet, skates
13	in, this, up, we	11	blades,
14	with	12	stick
15	helps, me	13	circles
16	move	14	puck, game
17	tells, when	17	coach
18	into	18	goal, net
20	every, work	19	player, job

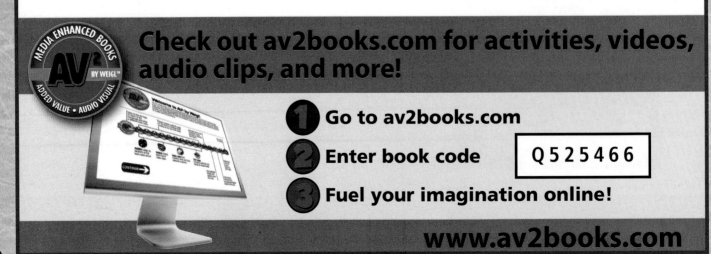

Check out av2books.com for activities, videos, audio clips, and more!

1 Go to av2books.com

2 Enter book code   Q 5 2 5 4 6 6

3 Fuel your imagination online!

www.av2books.com